LNAT ESSAY WRITING REVISION GUIDE BOOK: PREPARATION AND PRACTICE TESTS FOR SECTION B OF THE EXAM

LNAT (Law National Aptitude Test) is a registered trademark of the LNAT Consortium Ltd and is administered in partnership with Pearson VUE. Neither the LNAT Consortium nor Pearson VUE are affiliated with or endorse this publication.

LNAT Essay Writing Revision Guide Book: Preparation and Practice Tests for Section B of the Exam

© COPYRIGHT 2016 LNAT Success Associates

All rights reserved. No part of this publication may be reproduced, stored in a retrieval system, or transmitted, in any form or by any means, electronic, mechanical, photocopying, recording, or otherwise, without the prior written permission of the copyright owner.

ISBN-13:   978-1-949282-17-7
ISBN-10:   1-949282-17-1

NOTE: LNAT (Law National Aptitude Test) is a registered trademark of the LNAT Consortium Ltd and is administered in partnership with Pearson VUE. Neither the LNAT Consortium nor Pearson VUE are affiliated with or endorse this **publication**.

TABLE OF CONTENTS

Characteristics of the LNAT essay	1
Information on LNAT essay administration	3
The "Assertion-Argument-Counterargument-Synthesis-Conclusion" Essay Structure	4
Formulating Your Assertion	5
Supporting and Sustaining Your Argument	8
Acknowledging and Refuting the Counterargument	11
Extending and Elaborating Your Argument	14
Synthesizing the Viewpoints	16
Writing Your Conclusion	18
Sample essay 1	20
LNAT Essays: The key points summed up	23
Organizing your LNAT essay	24
What is 'argumentative language'?	26
Argumentative language exercise	26
Answer to argumentative language exercise	29
Using linking words and phrases effectively in your LNAT essay	32
Linking word exercise	37
Answers to the linking words exercise	40
Sample essay 2	40
Using adjectives to assert your opinion	43
Using adjectives - exercise	43
Answers to the adjective exercise	45
Using modality to argue your case	46
Modality exercise	46

Answers to the modality exercise	48
Using qualifiers to strengthen or limit your assertions	49
Qualifiers – exercise	49
Answers to the qualifiers exercise	50
Using verbs in the argument and counterargument	51
Verbs – exercise	51
List of verbs for the argument and counterargument	53
Answers to the verb exercise	55
Practice test 1 – section B	56
Answer to practice test 1 - sample essay 3	57
Analysis of essay structure in sample essay 3	60
Analysis of linking words and verbs in sample essay 3	62
Analysis of modality and qualifiers in sample essay 3	65
Practice test 2 – section B	68
Answer to practice test 2 - sample essay 4	69
Analysis of essay structure in sample essay 4	72
Analysis of linking words and verbs in sample essay 4	74
Analysis of modality and qualifiers in sample essay 4	77
Practice test 3 – section B	80
Answer to practice test 3 - sample essay 5	81
Analysis of essay structure in sample essay 5	84
Analysis of linking words and verbs in sample essay 5	87
Analysis of modality and qualifiers in sample essay 5	90
Practice test 4 – section B	93
Practice test 5 – section B	94

Characteristics of the LNAT Essay

Congratulations on your decision to study law. You are about to embark on an exciting and intellectually fulfilling period of your life.

In order to perform your best on the day of your LNAT test, you will need to prepare, and you have already taken steps towards doing that by getting this publication.

So, first of all, you need to know the answers to the following questions: why are you required to write an essay for the LNAT test and how do law schools use the essay to assess you as a potential candidate?

You are required to write an essay as part of the LNAT because law schools want to see if you have the necessary skills that are required of someone wanting to study law. These skills include:

- The ability to express your views clearly in writing
- The ability to evaluate and assess problems through logical thinking
- The ability to give reasons and justifications for your point of view
- The ability to anticipate objections to your viewpoints
- The ability to find weaknesses and contradictions in viewpoints that oppose your own
- The ability to synthesize what you see as the pros or cons of various courses of action in order to arrive at an optimal solution
- The ability to conclude or sum up an argument

It is important to understand that your essay will not be given a score or mark as often occurs in other standardized testing systems.

Rather, law schools will use your essay to see if it demonstrates the above skills. We will cover each one of these skills in this publication by giving you step-by-step instructions and exercises to help you focus on the 'nuts and bolts' of your argumentative writing.

It is highly recommended that you do the units in this publication in the order that they are given before viewing the sample essays at the end of the book.

Doing the units in this order will help you to assess your strengths and weaknesses more accurately as you work though the material.

Information on LNAT Essay Administration

On the day of your actual LNAT test, you will see three topics on the essay part of the test.

The essay part of the LNAT is in section B of the test.

You will be given 40 minutes to write your essay.

You will write your essay on a computer provided to you.

The computer will have a cut and paste function so that you will be able to edit your work efficiently.

The recommended length for your essay is 500 to 600 words, although essays may be up to a maximum of 750 words.

Assertion-Argument-Counterargument-Synthesis-Conclusion

The components of an argumentative essay are:

- Assertion

- Argument

- Counterargument

- Synthesis

- Conclusion

In this unit, we give definitions and explanations for the above concepts, discussing each one of these components in turn.

In the next unit, we discuss alternative ways to organize these components in your LNAT essay, depending upon the line of argument you decide to put forward.

Formulating Your Assertion

In general, an assertion is a statement of your point of view on a particular problem or topic. In your essay, you should normally make your primary assertion in the first paragraph. Your primary assertion should be a clear statement that responds to the specific point raised in the essay question. For instance, consider this essay question:

> *Countries which are heavily reliant upon motorized vehicles for transport would do well to establish governmental measures to promote the practice of using non-motorized vehicles. Discuss.*

You will notice that the essay question itself is already an assertion, so you need to first think about the pros and cons of the situation before formulating your primary assertion.

You can formulate your primary assertion by following these steps:

1. What are the advantages of the topic under discussion? In this case, the advantages of non-motorized transport include, among other things, the reduction of pollution, as well as health benefits to the general population (because people will walk and cycle more frequently).

2. Now think about the potential disadvantages. The general public often complain of living in a 'nanny state'. This phrase expresses

the idea that the government over-regulates day-to-day behaviours that should be left to common sense.

3. Finally, form a primary assertion for paragraph 1. Your primary assertion should indicate that you have an awareness that there is contention surrounding your position.

Remember that the first sentence of your LNAT essay needs to introduce your topic in a general way. You should put your primary assertion after the introductory sentence. So, a possible first paragraph for the above essay topic is as follows:

> There is a constant question in society nowadays about the environmental and health risks caused by the use of motorized vehicles. In spite of public complaints about the excessive involvement of the government in our private lives, it is irrefutable that increasing regulatory measures by a certain amount would bring about benefits to society.

You can also add a thesis statement at the end of your introductory paragraph. A thesis statement indicates how your essay is organized and gives a preview of the position you are going to take on the topic. Thesis statements often begin with the phrases 'This essay will discuss…' or 'I will show that…'.

In reality, though, a thesis statement is not really necessary for LNAT essays because you will have already indicated your position in your primary assertion sentence. In the above example, the writer's position is that his or her proposal 'would bring about benefits to society'.

If you prefer to add a thesis statement to your LNAT essay, the first paragraph would look something like this:

> There is a constant question in society nowadays about the environmental and health risks caused by the use of motorized vehicles. In spite of public complaints about the excessive involvement of the government in our private lives, it is irrefutable that increasing regulatory measures by a certain amount would bring about benefits to society. This essay will discuss the supporters and detractors to governmental involvement in the realm of traffic control, before describing two measures that the government might take to address the issue.

So, in the paragraph above, the thesis statement is as follows:

> This essay will discuss the supporters and detractors to governmental involvement in the realm of traffic control, before describing two measures that the government might take to address the issue.

Before moving on to the next section, we would be remiss if we did not point out that you will, of course, make many other assertions in your essay when you provide your supporting points.

However, remember that your essay will be the most effective when you begin with a strong statement of your overall position in your primary assertion in the first paragraph.

Supporting and Sustaining Your Argument

In an LNAT essay, an argument is when you provide reasons and examples to support your position.

- Remember that the essence of a good argument is that it gives persuasive and convincing reasons and examples to support its logical development.

- In other words, you need to provide valid points that logically support your position.

- You need to express your argument in a sustained and reasoned way, effectively using the argumentative language that is provided in one of the subsequent units in this material.

- In the subsequent units, we will also show you how to use other words and phrases to express and strengthen certain assertions that you make in your argument.

- You should note that, at times, you may, in fact, need to limit your assertions, depending upon the strength and validity of opposing views.

Now let's look again at our example essay topic and the first paragraph to the essay:

Countries which are heavily reliant upon motorized vehicles for transport would do well to establish governmental measures to promote the practice of using non-motorized vehicles. Discuss.

'There is a constant question in society nowadays about the environmental and health risks caused by the use of motorized vehicles. In spite of public complaints about the excessive involvement of the government in our private lives, it is irrefutable that increasing regulatory measures by a certain amount would bring about benefits to society'.

Because the primary assertion in the above paragraph is that 'increasing regulatory measures by a certain amount would bring about benefits to society', your argument should continue in the second paragraph by giving reasons for and examples of the benefits that will be derived from such a measure.

By continuing with the discussion of benefits, you ensure that your argument has a good 'line' or flow.

Achieving good flow will make your essay more persuasive and will also make it easier to read.

Now recall the advantages that we came up with when preparing our primary assertion. The advantages to governmental involvement in traffic control were:

1. The reduction of pollution
2. Health benefits to the general population because of more frequent walking and cycling.

Then decide which one of these advantages has more strength, in your opinion. Remember that an argument will be stronger when you can give evidence or examples to support it.

In this essay, we will use the health argument in the second paragraph, giving evidence from Denmark.

Here is a possible second paragraph for our essay topic:

> There is no doubt that countries using non-motorized transport as a norm have a better level of health in the general population. In Denmark, where most people cycle to work, it is reported that levels of heart disease and stroke are far lower than they are in other countries.

You can see that by backing up your assertion with a concrete example, like the one about Denmark above, you give your assertion more gravitas.

Acknowledging and Refuting the Counterargument

A counterargument is an objection or disadvantage to your proposed course of action.

- Just as with your argument, you will need to give reasons and examples to support the counterargument in order to demonstrate that you appreciate the validity of your opponent's concerns.
- If you do not do this, your essay might appear too simple or limited.
- When you express the counterargument, it will be beneficial to state it indirectly, using argumentative language.
- Using argumentative language will show that you understand the strength of your opponent's position, while distancing yourself from the opposing viewpoint.

For your convenience, we provide the second paragraph of the essay again below:

'There is no doubt that countries using non-motorized transport as a norm have a better level of health in the general population. In Denmark, where most people cycle to work, it is reported that levels of heart disease and stroke are far lower than they are in other countries'.

Notice that, up to this point, the second paragraph has spoken in support of your primary assertion, which is that 'increasing regulatory measures by a certain amount would bring about benefits to society'. Now we have to address the drawbacks to your primary assertion.

Recall the disadvantages that we mentioned when preparing our primary assertion. The disadvantages to governmental involvement in traffic control were:

1. The general public often complain of living in a 'nanny state'.
2. The government over-regulates day-to-day behaviours that should be left to common sense.

Bearing in mind these disadvantages, here is one possible way to continue the second paragraph of our essay:

> In spite of the health benefits, some would argue that cycling as a means of transport must be a matter left to personal choice. We constantly hear objections from the public about 'nanny-state' policies that cause unnecessary governmental intervention and bureaucracy in our lives. They claim the choice of whether or not to use an environmentally-friendly form of transport should be a matter of individual conscience. But we only have to consider the rising levels of environmental damage around the world to understand that personal choice and individual conscience as a means to improving the environment have, in fact, been ineffective thus far.

Notice the argumentative language ('some would argue that...' and 'They claim') in the first and third sentences. These phrases help to identify this response as a viewpoint that opposes your own.

You also place a distance between your own view and that of your opponent because you clearly identify the other side as 'some' and 'they'.

In addition to using argumentative language, you will normally come to some sort of resolution after you state the opposing viewpoint. Notice how the opposing viewpoint in the second paragraph is resolved by the final sentence:

> But we only have to consider the rising levels of environmental damage around the world to understand that personal choice and individual conscience as a means to improving the environment have, in fact, been ineffective thus far.

Such a resolution provides a good transition into the next paragraph of your essay and also serves to improve the flow or line of your writing.

Extending and Elaborating Your Argument

It is essential to understand that it will not be sufficient to give only one argument in your essay.

On a practical level, your essay has to be 500 words at a minimum, and it would be difficult to achieve that amount without giving a second argument.

More significantly, if you do not give a second argument and an elaboration of that second argument, your essay and your thinking will appear underdeveloped.

So, the next step is to think about how to extend your argument or line of reasoning in paragraph 3.

In the final part of paragraph 2, we talked about our opponent's view that there should be an element of personal choice in deciding to use alternative forms of transport. In essence, this belief in personal choice is the cornerstone of our opponent's view.

So, in the next part of the essay, we need to think about how to further advance our argument and undermine our opponent. In our sample essay on traffic control, we can undermine our opponent by finding flaws with the aspect of personal choice.

Think about countries where inhabitants do not always have the luxury of personally choosing to use an automobile, such as in the Far East. Then cite examples of countries where personal choice has led to excessive petrol consumption, such as in the United States.

Having planned our line of reasoning, here is a possible second argument for the third paragraph for our essay:

> One only needs to look at certain remote villages in the Far East, where the aspect of personal choice has been removed because motorized vehicles cannot be afforded. In doing so, one can see that levels of air pollution and other forms of environmental contamination are far less in these villages than in so-called 'developed' countries. Consider the converse case, for instance, in the United States, where a heavy reliance on motor vehicles has resulted in this country being one of the largest emitters of greenhouse gases in the world.

Note that it is not strictly necessary to attempt to refute your second argument by providing another counterargument from your opponent. In fact, sometimes giving another counterargument at this point would weaken your position.

In the example above, we provide the second argument about villages in the Far East. We then elaborate and strengthen that argument by citing a further example in the United States.

We also elaborate rather than counter-argue at this point because the idea of rising pollution levels was already mentioned in paragraph 2.

While this sample essay has two main arguments, please note that it is likely that you may even need to have a third argument in your essay in order to elaborate your ideas fully.

Synthesizing the Viewpoints

In your LNAT essay, your synthesis is where you continue to acknowledge your opponent's position, while showing that your primary assertion and arguments hold more sway than your opponent's viewpoint.

- A synthesis can simply consist of a strong reiteration of your primary assertion and the reasons why it still rings true.
- A synthesis can sometimes involve arriving at some sort of compromise between the opposing viewpoints.
- If you are going to offer a compromise, you need to state the specific conditions of it in your synthesis.

The following synthesis for our example essay includes a proposed compromise:

Therefore, it is evident that a compromise needs to be reached in order to balance the limitations on personal freedom that can result from imposing governmental control over the issue, on the one hand, while addressing the very exigent concerns of cleaning up the world's environment and promoting healthy habits amongst its inhabitants, on the other. After all, it is often stated that personal freedom of choice is the cornerstone of any democratic society.

Notice that the synthesis above uses the key words 'compromise' and 'in order to balance' to indicate clearly that a compromise is being proposed.

The balancing of opposing viewpoints is also signalled by the phrases 'on the one hand' and 'on the other'.

Writing Your Conclusion

The conclusion to your LNAT essay consists of your final comments, which need to indicate the proposition that you are putting forward in response to the issue at hand.

In other words, your conclusion needs to state the specific conditions of the outcome that you are proposing.

- You may need to re-state your position in your conclusion.

- Your conclusion is normally placed directly after the synthesis.

- The conclusion is often in the same paragraph as your synthesis.

- You may offer solutions to the issue at hand in your conclusion.

- Most importantly: Don't be noncommittal. Take a stand.

- Your essay will be viewed poorly if you say that both views have merit in general, but then you fail to state precisely what outcome you are advocating.

- In other words, avoid making a concluding remark such as: 'As you can see, there are pros and cons to both arguments, so it is difficult to find a resolution'.

The following conclusion for our example essay puts forward two possible solutions:

Perhaps the best solution to the issue at hand is to have the government provide certain incentives to those who decide not to use motorized vehicles. For instance, the government could offer rebates or subsidies on bicycle purchases. Another possible course of action would be to introduce certain governmental controls, but to establish those controls within very clear limits. Alternating car use by vehicle registration number has been an effective solution in certain countries. Under this scheme, car owners with odd-numbered registrations can use their vehicles on certain days of the week, while owners of vehicles with registrations ending in an even number are permitted to use their vehicles only on the other days. Violating this policy would result in a fine or other sanctions. To sum up, one thing is clear: whether by positive reinforcement, as in the first example, or by negative reinforcement as in the second, both remedies take into account the pressing concern of the state of the global environment, as well as protecting the need of the population for both personal health and individual freedom.

In the example above, two possible courses of action are put forward: one is an incentive plan, and the other is a plan involving fines and sanctions.

Notice how both courses of action are described precisely and with sufficient detail.

Closing your essay in this way leaves a positive impact on the person who is reading and evaluating it.

Sample Essay 1

We reproduce the entire example essay in full here so that you can see how the parts relate to each other and how it achieves a good line of argument.

> *'Countries which are heavily reliant upon motorized vehicles for transport would do well to establish governmental measures to promote the practice of using non-motorized vehicles'. Discuss.*

There is a constant question in society nowadays about the environmental and health risks caused by the use of motorized vehicles. In spite of public complaints about the excessive involvement of the government in our private lives, it is irrefutable that increasing regulatory measures by a certain amount would bring about benefits to society. This essay will discuss the supporters and detractors to governmental involvement in the realm of traffic control, before describing two measures that the government might take to address the issue.

There is no doubt that countries using non-motorized transport as a norm have a better level of health in the general population. In Denmark, where most people cycle to work, it is reported that levels of heart disease and stroke are far lower than they are in other countries. In spite of the health benefits, some would argue that cycling as a means of transport must be a matter left to personal choice. We constantly hear objections from the public about 'nanny-state' policies that cause unnecessary governmental intervention and bureaucracy in our lives. They claim the choice of whether or not to use an environmentally-friendly form of transport should be a matter of individual conscience. But we only have to consider the rising levels of environmental damage around the world to understand that personal choice and individual conscience as a means to improving the environment have, in fact, been ineffective thus far.

One only needs to look at certain remote villages in the Far East, where the aspect of personal choice has been removed because motorized vehicles cannot be afforded. In doing so, one can see that levels of air pollution and other forms of environmental contamination are far less in these villages than in so-called 'developed' countries. Consider the converse case, for instance, in the United States, where a heavy reliance on motor vehicles has resulted in this country being one of the largest emitters of greenhouse gases in the world.

Therefore, it is evident that a compromise needs to be reached in order to balance the limitations on personal freedom that can result from imposing governmental control over the issue, on the one hand, while addressing the very exigent concerns of cleaning up the world's environment and promoting healthy habits amongst its inhabitants, on the other. After all, it is often stated that personal freedom of choice is the cornerstone of any democratic society. Perhaps the best solution to the issue at hand is to have the government provide certain incentives to those who decide not to use motorized vehicles. For instance, the government could offer rebates or subsidies on bicycle purchases.

Another possible course of action would be to introduce certain governmental controls, but to establish those controls within very clear limits. Alternating car use by vehicle registration number has been an effective solution in certain countries. Under this scheme, car owners with odd-numbered registrations can use their vehicles on certain days of the week, while owners of vehicles with registrations ending in an even number are permitted to use their vehicles only on the other days. Violating this policy would result in a fine or other sanctions. To sum up, one thing is clear: whether by positive reinforcement, as in the first example, or by negative reinforcement as in the second, both remedies take into account the pressing concern of the state of the global environment, as well as protecting the need of the population for both personal health and individual freedom. [580 words]

LNAT Essays:
The Key Points Summed Up

So, to sum up our discussion, here's a brief list of key points to bear in mind when writing your LNAT essay.

How to argue your point:

- Answer the question with a primary assertion
- Provide a sustained line of argument
- Give evidence or examples to support it
- Address arguments which contradict your own line of argument
- Demonstrate a clear and convincing synthesis and conclusion to give a resolution to the essay and to take a stand.

Organizing Your LNAT Essay

We know that an LNAT essay contains the following elements: Assertion, Argument, Counterargument, Synthesis and Conclusion. However, you may have some doubt regarding how these individual elements should be organized. While the organization of your essay can vary depending on your writing skill and technique, as well as the essay theme, we believe that there are two particular organization schemes for the LNAT essay which are especially effective. They are as follows:

Scheme 1

- Assertion
- Argument 1
- Counterargument
- Argument 2
- Elaboration
- Synthesis
- Conclusion

A scheme 1 organizational style was used in the sample essay on non-motorized vehicles given in the previous section. When considering the amount and strength of existing counterarguments, however, it may be more beneficial in some cases to use the scheme 2 organizational style.

Scheme 2

- Assertion
- Argument 1
- Counterargument 1
- Argument 2
- Counterargument 2
- Synthesis
- Conclusion

As stated previously, it may be necessary in some cases to give more than two arguments and counterarguments; the above guidelines are offered by way of general advice on structure and organization.

We provide an example of an essay written using scheme 2 in sample essay 2 in this publication, which is on the theme of tourism.

What is 'Argumentative Language'?

In certain of the previous units in this publication, we have touched on the notion of 'argumentative language'.

'Argumentative language' means the words and phrases that you can use to introduce your own assertions and elaborations on those assertions.

You can also use argumentative language to introduce and distance yourself from opposing viewpoints.

Let's look at the argumentative language used in paragraph 1 of sample essay 1:

<u>There is a constant question</u> in society nowadays about the environmental and health risks caused by the use of motorized vehicles. In spite of public complaints about the excessive involvement of the government in our private lives, <u>it is irrefutable that</u> increasing regulatory measures <u>by a certain amount</u> would bring about benefits to society. This essay will discuss the supporters and detractors to this assertion, before describing two measures that the government might take to address the issue.

Exercise: *Now look at the reminder of sample essay 1 and underline the argumentative language. Please do not underline linking words (for example, because, in spite of, etc.) because we will analyse those in a later unit.*
The answer is provided on the pages immediately following this exercise.

There is no doubt that countries using non-motorized transport as a norm have a better level of health in the general population. In Denmark, where most people cycle to work, it is reported that levels of heart disease and stroke are far lower than they are in other countries. In spite of the health benefits, some would argue that cycling as a means of transport must be a matter left to personal choice. We constantly hear objections from the public about 'nanny-state' policies that cause unnecessary governmental intervention and bureaucracy in our lives. They claim the choice of whether or not to use an environmentally-friendly form of transport should be a matter of individual conscience. But we only have to consider the rising levels of environmental damage around the world to understand that personal choice and individual conscience as a means to improving the environment have, in fact, been ineffective thus far.

One only needs to look at certain remote villages in the Far East, where the aspect of personal choice has been removed because motorized vehicles cannot be afforded. In doing so, one can see that levels of air pollution and other forms of environmental contamination are far less in these villages than in so-called 'developed' countries. Consider the converse case, for instance, in the United States, where a heavy reliance on motor vehicles has resulted in this country being one of the largest emitters of greenhouse gases in the world.

Therefore, it is evident that a compromise needs to be reached in order to balance the limitations on personal freedom that can result from imposing governmental control over the issue, on the one hand, while addressing the very exigent concerns of cleaning up the world's environment and promoting healthy habits amongst its inhabitants, on the other. After all, it is often stated that personal freedom of choice is the cornerstone of any democratic society. Perhaps the best solution to the issue at hand is to have the government provide certain incentives to those who decide not to use motorized vehicles. For instance, the government could offer rebates or subsidies on bicycle purchases.

Another possible course of action would be to introduce certain governmental controls, but to establish those controls within very clear limits. Alternating car use by vehicle registration number has been an effective solution in certain countries. Under this scheme, car owners with odd-numbered registrations can use their vehicles on certain days of the week, while owners of vehicles with registrations ending in an even number are only permitted to use their vehicles on the other days. Violating this policy would result in a fine or other sanctions. To sum up, one thing is clear: whether by positive reinforcement, as in the first example, or by negative reinforcement as in the second, both remedies take into account the pressing concern of the state of the global environment, as well as protecting the need of the population for both personal health and individual freedom.

Answer to Argumentative Language Exercise

There is no doubt that countries using non-motorized transport as a norm have a better level of health in the general population. In Denmark, where most people cycle to work, it is reported that levels of heart disease and stroke are far lower than they are in other countries. In spite of the health benefits, some would argue that cycling as a means of transport must be a matter left to personal choice. We constantly hear objections from the public about 'nanny-state' policies that cause unnecessary governmental intervention and bureaucracy in our lives. They claim, the choice of whether or not to use an environmentally-friendly form of transport should be a matter of individual conscience. But we only have to consider the rising levels of environmental damage around the world to understand that personal choice and individual conscience as a means to improving the environment have, in fact, been ineffective thus far.

One only needs to look at certain remote villages in the Far East, where the aspect of personal choice has been removed because motorized vehicles cannot be afforded. In doing so, one can see that levels of air pollution and other forms of environmental contamination are far less in these villages than in so-called 'developed' countries. Consider the converse case, for instance, in the United States, a heavy reliance on motor vehicles has resulted in this country being one of the largest emitters of greenhouse gases in the world.

Therefore, it is evident that a compromise needs to be reached in order to balance the limitations on personal freedom that can result from imposing governmental control over the issue, on the one hand, while addressing the very exigent concerns of cleaning up the world's environment and promoting healthy habits amongst its inhabitants, on the other. After all, it is often stated that personal freedom of choice is the cornerstone of any democratic society. Perhaps the best solution to the issue at hand is to have the government provide certain incentives to those who decide not to use motorized vehicles. For instance, the government could offer rebates or subsidies on bicycle purchases.

Another possible course of action would be to introduce certain governmental controls, but to establish those controls within very clear limits. Alternating car use by vehicle registration number has been an effective solution in certain countries. Under this scheme, car owners with odd-numbered registrations can use their vehicles on certain days of the week, while owners of vehicles with registrations ending in an even number are only permitted to use their vehicles on the other days. Violating this policy would result in a fine or other sanctions. To sum up, one thing is clear: whether by positive reinforcement, as in the first example, or by negative reinforcement as in the second, both remedies take into account the pressing concern of the state of the global environment, as well as protecting the need of the population for both personal health and individual freedom.

Please notice that, depending on how you structure your essay, certain of the phrases above may be used to support your assertions, and alternatively the same phrases could be used to distance yourself from your opponent's claims. It's a matter of how cautious and diplomatic you want to be.

If the above exercise was a struggle for you, we recommend that you make a list of the above phrases and commit then to memory in order to use some of them in your essay on the day of your actual LNAT exam.

Using Linking Words and Phrases Effectively in Your LNAT Essay

The effective use of linking words and phrases will make your LNAT essay more organized, more persuasive and easier to read.

Unfortunately, problems can occur with punctuation and word placement when using linking words and phrases. Of course, in order to make the best impact with your LNAT essay, you should be sure to observe the conventions of correct grammar and punctuation.

Linking words and phrases (also known as discursive markers) fall into three categories. Please read the following rules for word placement and punctuation for each category:

1) The first category of linking words and phrases is the <u>sentence linker</u>. Sentence linkers are usually placed at the beginning of a sentence and are followed by a comma.

Look at this example of using a sentence linker at the start of the sentence:

However, you should still study hard.

For emphasis, you can use sentence linkers in the middle of a sentence. If you do so, be sure that you put commas both before and after the sentence linker. Now look at this example to see how a sentence linker is used in the middle of a sentence of the sentence:

You should, *however*, still study hard.

2) The second category of linking words and phrases is the <u>phrase linker</u>. Phrase linkers must be followed by a noun or noun phrase (a phrase does not contain a verb).

Phrase linkers should not be followed by a clause (a clause contains at least one verb).

Now look at this phrase linker example:

> He passed the exam *because of* his preparation.

'His preparation' is a noun phrase. In other words, it does not contain a verb. Remember that verbs are words that show action.

3) The third category of linking words and phrases is the <u>subordinator</u>. Subordinators must be followed by a clause. Subordinators should not be followed by a phrase.

Again, remember that clauses must contain at least one verb.

Here is a subordinator example:

> *Although* he worked hard, he failed to make his business successful.

'Although' is a subordinator. In the above example sentence 'he worked hard' is a clause. The verb is 'worked.'

On the following pages, we provide a list of the most common linking words and phrases, grouped according to their category. Note which ones are sentence linkers, which ones are phrase linkers, and which ones are subordinators. You will use these words and phrases in the exercise that follows the list.

Linking Words and Phrases:

<u>Sentence linkers for giving additional information</u>

further

furthermore

apart from this

what is more

in addition

additionally

in the same way

moreover

<u>Sentence linkers for giving examples</u>

for example

for instance

firstly / first of all

in this case

in particular

mainly

more precisely

namely

in brief / in short

in essence

<u>Phrase linkers for giving specific information</u>

particularly

especially

specifically

<u>Sentence linkers for stating the obvious</u>

obviously

clearly

naturally

of course

surely

after all

<u>Phrase linkers for giving generalizations</u>

in general

on the whole

as a rule

for the most part

generally speaking

in most cases

Sentence linkers for stating causes and effects

thus

accordingly

hence

therefore

in that case

under those circumstances

as a result

for this reason

as a consequence

consequently

in effect

Phrase linkers for stating causes and effects

because of

Subordinator for stating causes and effects

because

Sentence linkers for showing contrast

on the other hand

on the contrary

alternatively

rather

otherwise

Phrase linker for showing contrast

in contrast to

Sentence linkers for showing similarity

similarly

in the same way

likewise

Phrase linker for showing similarity

just as

Sentence linkers for paraphrasing or restating

in other words

that is to say

that is

Subordinators	Sentence linkers for concession or unexpected results
after	
although	however
as	nevertheless
before	still
even though	yet
if	meanwhile
since	**Phrase linkers for concession or unexpected results**
so / so that	
that	despite
unless	in spite of
until	but rather
when	**Sentence linkers for giving conclusions**
while	
whereas	finally
not only . . . but also	to conclude
as well as	lastly
besides	in conclusion

Exercise: *Read the essay that follows and place the linking words or phrases provided below into the correct gaps. When you have finished, compare your answers to those in sample essay 2.*

for instance / hence / although / because / because of / not only / but also / yet / further / first of all / even though / nevertheless / in addition / however

Tourism brings more harm than good to the poorer countries of the world. Discuss.

Cheaper flights are making it more and more affordable and convenient for people around the world to travel to other countries. In the UK alone, there has been a recent proliferation in low-cost and budget airlines, which has made it easier for the average family to afford a holiday to some 'exotic' destination. _____ , in many cases, 'exotic' may mean one of the less economically well-off countries of the world. Sometimes having less infrastructure and being removed from the hustle and bustle of the holidaymaker's normal life, these destinations are selected because they are seen as holding a restorative balm to modern life's daily stresses. _____ such holidays may be beneficial for the holidaymaker, the negative effects of the increasing throngs of tourists on the poorer countries of the world should give us reason to take pause _____ it is clear that there are problems associated with the expanding global tourism industry.

Apart from the obvious environmental damage that tourism causes, _____ , we must consider increasing crime rates. Some local residents might see tourists as easy prey because, _____ are they in unfamiliar territory and therefore less able to take care of themselves, _____ because they carry visible items of wealth such as jewellery and electronic equipment, which can be readily resold for a quick profit. _____, holidaymakers might argue in response to this claim that they know how to protect themselves, so there is no danger. Some might even claim that they leave all valuables home when travelling abroad. _____,such arguments focus merely on theft, without taking in account other crimes. _____, some people will knowingly purchase illegal copies of films from a shop abroad that sells pirated copies of digital goods. Believing that the authorities turn a blind eye to such 'soft' crimes, normally law-abiding tourists behave in this way because they realize that they can do so with impunity. Consider the even more extreme case of tourists who go abroad to take advantage of that country's lack of enforcement of recreational drug use or prostitution. _____ recreational drugs and prostitution are illegal in certain of these countries, some tourists again believe that they can justify their actions merely because of the fact that they will escape punishment. _____, these tourists fail to consider that these crimes are not enforced because of the country's economic conditions in the first place, and that by participating in these crimes, they are exacerbating and perpetuating crime even further in the host country.

_____, another major problem is healthcare. With greater mobility comes greater danger of spreading contagious diseases. On a local level, tourists' illnesses, accidents and injuries place a strain on local healthcare systems and in extreme cases can threaten the lives of the local people who are unaccustomed to certain strains of diseases. Holidaymakers might claim that they would not consider travelling when they are under the weather. _____, others might argue that they never travel without getting a medical insurance policy for their trips. Nevertheless, the flaws in these arguments can easily be revealed: people can carry strains of bacteria-causing illnesses without feeling unwell, and regardless of whether one is in possession of a medical insurance policy or not, he or she might require a stay in a local hospital _____ the illness or injury, thereby putting further strain on local resources.

These are just two reasons why tourism can do more harm than good. These phenomena suggest that one should devote careful awareness to his or her selection of a tourist destination by taking into consideration the effects of one's proposed trip on the host country. All in all, it might appear that 'voluntourism' will become more popular in the future if the general public takes the needs of the host country into account when deciding where to go on holiday.

Sample Essay 2

Tourism brings more harm than good to the poorer countries of the world. Discuss.

Cheaper flights are making it more and more affordable and convenient for people around the world to travel to other countries. In the UK alone, there has been a recent proliferation in low-cost and budget airlines, which has made it easier for the average family to afford a holiday to some 'exotic' destination. However, in many cases, 'exotic' may mean one of the less economically well-off countries of the world. Sometimes having less infrastructure and being removed from the hustle and bustle of the holidaymaker's normal life, these destinations are selected because they are seen as holding a restorative balm to modern life's daily stresses. Although such holidays may be beneficial for the holidaymaker, the negative effects of the increasing throngs of tourists on the poorer countries of the world should give us reason to take pause because it is clear that there are problems associated with the expanding global tourism industry.

Apart from the obvious environmental damage that tourism causes, first of all, we must consider increasing crime rates. Some local residents might see tourists as easy prey because, not only are they in unfamiliar territory and therefore less able to take care of themselves, but also because they carry visible items of wealth such as jewellery and electronic equipment, which can be readily resold for a quick profit. Nevertheless, holidaymakers might argue in response to this claim that they know how to protect themselves, so there is no danger. Some might even claim that they leave all valuables home when travelling abroad. Yet, such arguments focus merely on theft, without taking in account other crimes. For instance, some people will knowingly purchase illegal copies of films from a shop abroad that sells pirated copies of digital goods. Believing that the authorities turn a blind eye to such 'soft' crimes, normally law-abiding tourists behave in this way because they realize that they can do so with impunity. Consider the even more extreme case of tourists who go abroad to take advantage of that country's lack of enforcement of recreational drug use or prostitution. Even though recreational drugs and prostitution are illegal in certain of these countries, some tourists again believe that they can justify their actions merely because of the fact that they will escape punishment. Hence, these tourists fail to consider that these crimes are not enforced because of the country's economic conditions in the first place, and that by participating in these crimes, they are exacerbating and perpetuating crime even further in the host country.

In addition, another major problem is healthcare. With greater mobility comes greater danger of spreading contagious diseases. On a local level, tourists' illnesses, accidents and injuries place a strain on local healthcare systems and in extreme cases can threaten the lives of the local people who are unaccustomed to certain strains of diseases. Holidaymakers might claim that they would not consider travelling when they are under the weather. <u>Further</u>, others might argue that they never travel without getting a medical insurance policy for their trips. Nevertheless, the flaws in these arguments can easily be revealed: people can carry strains of bacteria-causing illnesses without feeling unwell, and regardless of whether one is in possession of a medical insurance policy or not, he or she might require a stay in a local hospital <u>because of</u> the illness or injury, thereby putting further strain on local resources.

These are just two reasons why tourism can do more harm than good. These phenomena suggest that one should devote careful awareness to his or her selection of a tourist destination by taking into consideration the effects of one's proposed trip on the host country. All in all, it might appear that 'voluntourism' will become more popular in the future if the general public takes the needs of the host country into account when deciding where to go on holiday. [633 words]

Please note that you can interchange positions of the following words:

However / Nevertheless / Yet

Although / Even though

In addition / Further

Using Adjectives to Assert Your Opinion

Adjectives are words that are used to describe nouns. You should use adjectives in your LNAT essay to strengthen and intensify your assertions, as well as and to weaken or limit your opponent's claims.

- Remember that a noun can normally be classified as a person, place or thing.
- For example, in the sentence 'Science is a boring subject' the word 'boring' is an adjective and the word 'subject' is a thing.

Now look at these two sentences:

The present rate of global warming is a problem in the world today.

The present rate of global warming is an exigent problem in the world today.

The second sentence is much more persuasive than the first because it uses the adjective 'exigent' to emphasize that the problem is extremely urgent or pressing.

Exercise: *Look at the following sentences and underline the adjectives that the writer uses to advance her assertions. Then make a mental note of these adjectives so that you can use them in your LNAT essay. The answers are provided on the following page.*

1) Britain's history is its greatest asset.
2) The landscape is an integral part of our identity.
3) Our heritage is fundamental to our culture.

4) Accepting change is a critical part of making decisions.

5) This decision is of paramount importance.

6) Listed buildings are a key part of our culture.

7) Clear policies on this issue are essential.

Answers to the Adjective Exercise

1) Britain's history is its <u>greatest</u> asset.

2) The landscape is an <u>integral</u> part of our identity.

3) Our heritage is <u>fundamental</u> to our culture.

4) Accepting change is a <u>critical</u> part of making decisions.

5) This decision is of <u>paramount</u> importance.

6) Listed buildings are a <u>key</u> part of our culture.

7) <u>Clear</u> policies on this issue are <u>essential</u>.

Using Modality to Argue Your Case

When we talk about 'modality' in a grammatical sense, we are referring to the use of modal verbs in writing.

- Modal verbs include the following: can, could, may, must, ought to, shall, should, would, have to
- Modal verbs are extremely useful in LNAT essays because they can be used to help express your assertions and strengthen your examples.
- Modal verbs can also be used to limit the intensity of the opposing viewpoint.
- Remember that you can use modal verbs in either the affirmative or negative form.
- For example, 'should' is the affirmative form, while 'should not' is the negative form.

Exercise: *Place the correct modal verb in the sentence below from the options provided at the end of each sentence. Notice that in some sentences, both options are correct. When both options are correct, please state which option strengthens the assertion the most. The answers are provided on the following page.*

1) We _____ not hide our heritage. (should / have to)

2) We do not _____ look far to encounter this phenomenon. (have to / must)

3) We _____ not make that decision arbitrarily. (must / should)

4) We _____ work together to achieve this aim. (shall / could)

5) We _____ protect the environment. (would / ought to)

Answers to Modality Exercise

1) We _____ not hide our heritage. (should / have to)

   The correct answer is 'should'.

   In order to use 'have to', the word order would be different: We do not have to hide our heritage.

2) We do not _____ look far to encounter this phenomenon. (have to / must)

   The correct answer is 'have to'. Must is incorrect grammatically.

3) We _____ not make that decision arbitrarily. (must / should)

   Both answers are correct. 'Must' is stronger than 'should' in this case because it is used to expresses a strong obligation, rather than a recommendation (as in the case of 'should' in this sentence).

4) We _____ work together to achieve this aim. (shall / could)

   Both answers are correct. 'Shall' is stronger than 'could' because it expresses a future intention, rather than a mere possibility.

5) We _____ protect the environment. (would / ought to)

   The correct answer is 'ought to'. 'Would' does not provide the correct sense to the sentence.

Using Qualifiers to Strengthen or Limit Your Assertions

'Qualify' means limit or modify, particularly to modify the meaning of a word or phrase. Qualifiers are words that can be used in your LNAT essay either to make your assertions sound more serious or to advance your own arguments.

- Qualifiers can also be used to acknowledge your opponent's viewpoints (which, of course, you will then go on to refute).
- Qualifiers often include words that can be used as adverbs, such as: surely, fairly, allegedly
- Remember that, to make a very broad grammatical generalization, adverbs often end with the letters –ly.

Exercise*: Imagine that you are writing an argumentative essay that puts forward your argument that the government's economic policies and proposals are largely ineffectual. Please underline the qualifier in each sentence. Then state whether the qualifier is being used to advance your own argument or whether the qualifier is being used to acknowledge your opponent's viewpoints.*

1) Admittedly, the government's plans have some redeeming features.
2) This economic policy has been rightly criticized.
3) There are certainly advantages to this economic proposal.
4) Equally there are arguments against the proposal.
5) However, policy and reality are often mutually exclusive.

Answers to the Qualifiers Exercise

1) <u>Admittedly</u>, the government's plans have some redeeming features.

   You will recall that your argument is that the government's economic policies and proposals are largely ineffectual. So, the qualifier in the sentence above is being used to acknowledge your opponent's viewpoints.

2) This economic policy has been <u>rightly</u> criticized.

   Used to advance your own argument

3) There are <u>certainly</u> advantages to this economic proposal.

   Used to acknowledge your opponent's viewpoints

4) <u>Equally</u> there are arguments against the proposal.

   Used to advance your own argument

5) However, policy and reality are often <u>mutually</u> exclusive.

   Used to advance your own argument

Using Verbs in the Argument and Counterargument

As stated previously in our discussion of linking words and phrases, verbs are words that show action. Practice how to use verbs to your advantage in your LNAT essay by completing the exercise below.

Exercise: Sample essay 2 was an argumentative essay querying whether tourism brings more harm than good to the poorer counties of the world. Some sentences from that essay are reproduced below. Look at the list of useful argumentative verbs and verb phrases on the page following the exercise. Then read the sentences below and underline all of the argumentative verb forms in each sentence. Note that you should not identify every verb, but rather only the argumentative ones. The answers to the exercises are given on the page following the verb list.

1) Nevertheless, holidaymakers might argue in response to this claim that they know how to protect themselves, so there is no danger.

2) Some might even claim that they leave all valuables home when travelling abroad.

3) Yet, such arguments focus merely on theft, without taking in account other crimes.

4) Believing that the authorities turn a blind eye to such 'soft' crimes, normally law-abiding tourists behave in this way because they realize that they can do so with impunity.

5) Consider the even more extreme case of tourists who go abroad to take advantage of that country's lack of enforcement of recreational drug use or prostitution.

6) Even though recreational drugs and prostitution are illegal in certain of these countries, some tourists again believe that they can justify their actions merely because of the fact that they will escape punishment.

7) Hence, these tourists fail to consider that these crimes are not enforced because of the country's economic conditions in the first place, and that by participating in these crimes, they are exacerbating and perpetuating crime even further in the host country.

Useful Verbs for the Argument and Counterargument

address
afford (meaning: provide)
agree
approach
argue
assert
assume
believe
challenge
claim
coerce
comment
conclude
consider
concede
contend
contradict
convince

demonstrate
deny
disagree
discern
dispute
emphasize
enumerate
exacerbate
hasten
hold / hold the view
imply
infer
influence
maintain
perpetrate
perpetuate
persuade
peruse

point out	report
ponder	repudiate
propose	reveal
protect	say
qualify	state
query	suggest
question	sum up
realize	stipulate
recognize	take heed
recommend	take into account
refute	view
reject	value
remark	warn

Answers to the Verb Exercise

1) Nevertheless, holidaymakers might <u>argue</u> in response to this claim that they know how to protect themselves, so there is no danger.

2) Some might even <u>claim</u> that they leave all valuables home when travelling abroad.

3) Yet, such arguments focus merely on theft, <u>without taking in account</u> other crimes.

4) <u>Believing</u> that the authorities turn a blind eye to such 'soft' crimes, normally law-abiding tourists behave in this way because they <u>realize</u> that they can do so with impunity.

5) <u>Consider</u> the even more extreme case of tourists who go abroad to take advantage of that country's lack of enforcement of recreational drug use or prostitution.

6) Even though recreational drugs and prostitution are illegal in certain of these countries, some tourists again <u>believe</u> that they can justify their actions merely because of the fact that they will escape punishment.

7) Hence, these tourists fail to <u>consider</u> that these crimes are not enforced because of the country's economic conditions in the first place, and that by participating in these crimes, they are <u>exacerbating</u> and <u>perpetuating</u> crime even further in the host country.

LNAT Practice Test 1

Section B: Essay

Now that you have completed the review exercises, you should attempt the following practice tests. Remember to allow 40 minutes to take each test. A model response to question 3 is provided in the next section.

Answer ONE of the following questions.

You must substantiate your argument with persuasive reasons and examples which justify your point of view.

1. All immigrants wishing to reside permanently in the United Kingdom should be required to show evidence of English language proficiency. Do you agree?

2. Society should assume more responsibility for pregnant teenagers and the children they bear. Do you agree?

3. Advertising serves only to manipulate the public, rather than to provide information. Do you agree?

Sample Essay 3

This essay is in response to essay question 3 from practice test 1 on the previous page. A detailed analysis of the essay is provided after the written essay response.

Advertising serves only to manipulate the public, rather than to provide information. Do you agree?

Advertising is a powerful force in today's materialistic, status-conscious society. Consumers are bombarded with advertising at every turn, from advertisements on television and radio, to outdoor advertising on electronic signs and even on buses. The abundance of advertising that confronts a person from one day to the next thus leaves one to wonder: How much of this advertising is really useful or necessary? This essay will reveal that while the majority of advertising serves only to drive mindless consumerism, a certain form of advertising does, in fact, serve a useful purpose.

Most advertising that we see nowadays, especially that on television, is the attempt of large companies to persuade the general public to buy products that they do not need, and may not ultimately want. In other words, advertisements do not truly exist to give product information to consumers, but rather to coerce them mentally into buying the product in question. Further, I would argue that this phenomenon has larger economic repercussions because it creates a false economy in which a demand is created for goods that are not really necessary. One only has to consider the amount of advertising for toys during children's TV programmes to see this phenomenon in action. Perhaps the false economy created in this case is even more dreadful than it is normally, because it incites the demand for the product in question in children, who do not have the intellectual and developmental savvy to appreciate that they are being manipulated.

However, detractors to this viewpoint would claim that advertising nevertheless does provide information about products to consumers. They assert that, rather than producing a false economy, the practice of advertising helps to perpetuate competition and free enterprise in the marketplace and ultimately brings the best prices to customers. Under this view, advertising helps to sell goods to a larger market; therefore, as more goods are sold to the public, they become cheaper since they can be mass produced in order to meet demand.

But again, even a superficial analysis of this argument reveals that it is based on at least two obvious fallacies. First of all, sometimes the 'information' provided in advertising is based on scant evidence, which is paraded as empirical proof in order to convince the consumer to buy. Take the advertising of cosmetics as a case in point. By now, many people will have seen the advertisement on UK television that states that 76% of the women tested felt that their wrinkles appeared to be visibly reduced after using a certain brand of face cream. Notice how carefully and manipulatively the advertisement is worded: 'the women tested *felt* that their wrinkles *appeared* to be *visibly* reduced'. The advertisement doesn't state that the condition of the women's skin actually improved from using the product. Notably, the 'low price' argument also fails in this case as the women are encouraged to pay more for the product 'because they're worth it'.

Although I have enumerated what I see as the evils of advertising, I might be remiss if I did not concede that there is one case in which advertising does serve an extremely valuable purpose. I am speaking here about public service advertisements like those that warn against the dangers of driving while intoxicated or failing to wear a seat belt. Admittedly, these kinds of advertisements can literally have a very sobering effect.

So, what is the future of advertising? Should the government intervene to stamp down on the false or misleading claims that some advertisers attempt to make? It does in fact appear that a sea change may be beginning to take place already. For instance, some TV and magazine advertisements are now required to display footnotes at the bottom of the screen or page in order to qualify their claims. Providing information like this that clearly states the true limitations of products can only have a salutary effect. [647 words]

Analysis of Essay Structure in Sample Essay 3

First we will analyse the structure of the essay and the argumentative language the essay uses. On the following pages, we will analyse the writer's use of linking words, adjectives, modality, qualifiers and verbs.

This essay uses a 'scheme 1' organizational scheme.

Assertion – The primary assertion is in the last sentence of paragraph 1: 'while the majority of advertising serves only to drive mindless consumerism, a certain form of advertising does, in fact, serve a useful purpose'.

The argumentative language from this paragraph is: 'the abundance of' and 'How much of …is really useful or necessary?'

Argument 1 – The writer's first argument is in paragraph 2. It is that advertising 'persuade[s] the general public to buy products that they do not need' and thereby creates a 'false economy'.

The argumentative language from this paragraph is: 'I would argue that' and 'One only has to consider'.

Counterargument 1 – Counterargument 1 is in paragraph 3. It is that advertising is necessary because it 'provide[s] information about products to consumers' and 'brings the best prices' to them.

The argumentative language from this paragraph is: 'detractors to this viewpoint would claim that', 'They assert that' and 'under this view'.

Argument 2 – Argument 2 is in paragraph 4. It is that sometimes the information provided in advertising is misleading and that sometimes companies actually increase the price of their product.

The argumentative language from this paragraph is: an 'analysis of this argument reveals that it is based on …fallacies' and 'Take … as a case in point'. In the fifth paragraph, the writer makes an exception for public service advertising.

Synthesis – The synthesis of the essay is found in the two rhetorical questions: 'So, what is the future of advertising?' and 'Should the government intervene to stamp down on the false or misleading claims that some advertisers attempt to make?'

Conclusion – The writer's conclusion is: 'Providing information like this that clearly states the true limitations of products can only have a salutary effect'.

Analysis of Linking Words and Verbs in Sample Essay 3

As stated in the units at the beginning of this publication, you can use linking words, adjectives, modality, qualifiers and verbs to make your LNAT essay more effective. Pay particular attention to the highlighted **linking words**, *adjectives* and <u>verbs</u> in sample essay 3 below.

Advertising is a *powerful* force in today's materialistic, status-conscious society. Consumers are bombarded with advertising at every turn, from advertisements on television and radio, to outdoor advertising on electronic signs and even on buses. The abundance of advertising that confronts a person from one day to the next **thus** leaves one to wonder: How much of this advertising is really *useful* or *necessary*? This essay will <u>reveal</u> that **while** the majority of advertising serves only to drive *mindless* consumerism, a certain form of advertising does, **in fact**, serve a useful purpose.

Most advertising that we see nowadays, especially that on television, is the attempt of large companies to <u>persuade</u> the general public to buy products that they do not need, and may not ultimately want. **In other words**, advertisements do not truly exist to give product information to consumers, **but rather** to <u>coerce</u> them mentally into buying the product in question. **Further**, I would argue that this phenomenon has larger economic repercussions **because** it creates a false economy in which a demand is created for goods that are not really necessary.

One only has to consider the amount of advertising for toys during children's TV programmes to see this phenomenon in action. Perhaps the false economy created in this case is even more *dreadful* than it is normally, **because** it incites the demand for the product in question in children, who do not have the intellectual and developmental savvy to appreciate that they are being manipulated.

However, detractors to this viewpoint would <u>claim</u> that advertising **nevertheless** does provide information about products to consumers. They <u>assert</u> that, **rather than** producing a false economy, the practice of advertising helps to <u>perpetuate</u> competition and free enterprise in the marketplace and ultimately brings the best prices to customers. **Under this view,** advertising helps to sell goods to a larger market; **therefore**, as more goods are sold to the public, they become cheaper **since** they can be mass produced in order to meet demand.

Yet again, even a superficial analysis of this argument reveals that it is based on at least two *obvious* fallacies. **First of all**, sometimes the 'information' provided in advertising is based on *scant* evidence, which is paraded as empirical proof in order to <u>convince</u> the consumer to buy. Take the advertising of cosmetics as a case in point. By now, many people will have seen the advertisement on UK television that states that 76% of the women tested felt that their wrinkles appeared to be visibly reduced after using a certain brand of face cream. Notice how carefully and manipulatively the advertisement is worded: 'the women tested felt that their wrinkles appeared to be visibly reduced'. The advertisement doesn't <u>state</u> that the condition of the women's skin actually improved from using the product. Notably, the 'low price' argument **also** fails in this case **as** the women are encouraged to pay more for the product 'because they're worth it'.

Although I have enumerated what I see as the evils of advertising, I might be remiss if I did not <u>concede</u> that there is one case in which advertising does serve an extremely *valuable* purpose. I am speaking here about public service advertisements like those that <u>warn against</u> the dangers of driving while intoxicated or failing to wear a seat belt. Admittedly, these kinds of advertisements can literally have a very sobering effect.

So, what is the future of advertising? Should the government intervene to stamp down on the false or misleading claims that some advertisers attempt to make? It does **in fact** appear that a sea change may be beginning to take place already. **For instance**, some TV and magazine advertisements are now required to display footnotes at the bottom of the screen or page in order to <u>qualify</u> their claims. Providing information like this that clearly states the true limitations of products can only have a *salutary* effect.

Analysis of Modality and Qualifiers in Sample Essay 3

Now look at essay 3 again, noting the use of <u>modality</u> and **qualifiers**.

Advertising is a powerful force in today's materialistic, status-conscious society. Consumers are bombarded with advertising at every turn, from advertisements on television and radio, to outdoor advertising on electronic signs and even on buses. The abundance of advertising that confronts a person from one day to the next thus leaves one to wonder: How much of this advertising is really useful or necessary? This essay will reveal that while the majority of advertising serves only to drive mindless consumerism, a certain form of advertising does, in fact, serve a useful purpose.

Most advertising that we see nowadays, especially that on television, is the attempt of large companies to persuade the general public to buy products that they do not need, and <u>may</u> not ultimately want. In other words, advertisements do not truly exist to give product information to consumers, but rather to coerce them mentally into buying the product in question. Further, I <u>would</u> argue that this phenomenon has larger economic repercussions because it creates a false economy in which a demand is created for goods that are not really necessary. One only has to consider the amount of advertising for toys during children's TV programmes to see this phenomenon in action. Perhaps the false economy created in this case is even more dreadful than it is normally, because it incites the demand for the product in question in children, who do not have the intellectual and developmental savvy to appreciate that they are being manipulated.

However, detractors to this viewpoint would claim that advertising nevertheless does provide information about products to consumers. They assert that, rather than producing a false economy, the practice of advertising helps to perpetuate competition and free enterprise in the marketplace and ultimately brings the best prices to customers. Under this view, advertising helps to sell goods to a larger market; therefore, as more goods are sold to the public, they become cheaper since they can be mass produced in order to meet demand.

Yet again, even a superficial analysis of this argument reveals that it is based on at least two obvious fallacies. First of all, sometimes the 'information' provided in advertising is based on scant evidence, which is paraded as empirical proof in order to convince the consumer to buy. Take the advertising of cosmetics as a case in point. By now, many people will have seen the advertisement on UK television that states that 76% of the women tested felt that their wrinkles appeared to be visibly reduced after using a certain brand of face cream. Notice how carefully and manipulatively the advertisement is worded: 'the women tested felt that their wrinkles appeared to be visibly reduced'. The advertisement doesn't state that the condition of the women's skin actually improved from using the product. **Notably**, the 'low price' argument also fails in this case as the women are encouraged to pay more for the product 'because they're worth it'.

Although I have enumerated what I see as the evils of advertising, I <u>might</u> be remiss if I did not concede that there is one case in which advertising does serve an extremely valuable purpose. I am speaking here about public service advertisements like those that warn against the dangers of driving while intoxicated or failing to wear a seat belt. **Admittedly**, these kinds of advertisements <u>can</u> literally have a very sobering effect.

So, what is the future of advertising? <u>Should</u> the government intervene to stamp down on the false or misleading claims that some advertisers attempt to make? It does in fact appear that a sea change <u>may</u> be beginning to take place already. For instance, some TV and magazine advertisements are now required to display footnotes at the bottom of the screen or page in order to qualify their claims. Providing information like this that clearly states the true limitations of products <u>can</u> only have a salutary effect.

LNAT Practice Test 2

Section B: Essay

Allow 40 minutes to take this test. A model response to question 2 is provided in the next section.

Answer ONE of the following questions.

You must substantiate your argument with persuasive reasons and examples which justify your point of view.

1. Marijuana should be fully legalized. Do you agree?

2. The internet provides too much unreliable, useless information. Discuss

3. What is your response to the view that the government should intervene to regulate cosmetic surgery?

Sample Essay 4

This essay is in response to essay question 2 from practice test 2 on the previous page. A detailed analysis of the essay is provided after the written essay response.

The internet provides too much unreliable, useless information. Discuss

In today's digital and electronic age, it almost goes without question that the internet is practical for our daily lives because it makes some mundane tasks more convenient. For instance, gone are the days when one had to go to the travel agent and sit in front of a desk while the agent looked through offers on his or her screen. Internet users can now book airline tickets and make travel arrangements in the comfort of their own living rooms with the click of a mouse. But in spite of the numerous conveniences of the internet, there are those who hold the view that the internet contains a great deal of worthless, harmful and offensive information and that the internet can be used to perpetrate deception and even crime. It appears that although the internet can be a useful tool in many ways, it needs to be used cautiously, and should even be regulated, in some circumstances.

It is an undeniable facet of modern life that the internet is useful for our communication needs and for making social contacts. Remember the days when one had to post a letter to communicate with someone overseas? Those days are in the past now thanks to the wonder of electronic mail, instant messaging, chat-rooms, forums and social networking sites. Still, others would maintain that often these social contacts are the breeding ground for dishonest or even criminally-minded individuals who want to prey on the weak and vulnerable. We have heard numerous stories of adolescents who are lured away from home to meet someone that they have communicated with online. Regrettably, in the end, the person making contact turns out to be a sexual predator intent on harming the young person. Such an experience, certainly, would negatively influence the child during the formative years of his or her personality development.

In addition to the double-edged sword effect of the communications capabilities of the internet, there is no disputing that the internet gives us ready access to a great deal of information. Indeed, some websites contain indispensable factual information for daily life and health. Consider the case of someone who wants to quit smoking. He or she can go to websites like the one run by the NHS to get the help and support needed to give up. Many of these types of websites are established by governmental agencies or charitable organizations, so the user can be confident that the information contained on these sites is trustworthy. On the other hand, however, one must also concede that much of the so-called 'information' on the internet needs to be read with a critical mind. Since anyone can set up a website, the qualifications of the site owner, as well as the accuracy and quality of the information on the site need to be perused sceptically. The rise of medical forums run by people with no medical training whatsoever and the abundance of online shops selling discount medications are a particular worry, as some people will rely on these websites to make a self-diagnosis and then purchase medicine, without taking heed of the possibility that the medicine could potentially kill them.

Yet, others would suggest that the media has seriously exaggerated the number of incidents of internet users being grievously harmed or killed by people they have met or products they have purchased on the internet and that the very large majority of the population have the common sense to know what is dangerous or not. But what about the minority of people who do not? Will they remain unprotected just to accommodate the desires of the majority? It is true that internet usage needs to be approached vigilantly on certain occasions. The internet will need to face governmental regulation in the future, but that regulation will need to be moderate, because if the internet becomes too highly regulated, it will lose a great deal of the convenience that it already affords us. [656 words]

Analysis of Essay Structure in Sample Essay 4

As before, we will analyse the structure of the essay and the argumentative language the essay uses. On the following pages, we will analyse the writer's use of linking words, adjectives, modality, qualifiers and verbs.

This essay uses a 'scheme 2' organizational scheme.

Assertion – The primary assertion is in the last sentence of paragraph 1: 'while … the internet can be a useful tool in many ways, it needs to be used cautiously, and should even be regulated, in some circumstances'.

The argumentative language from this paragraph is: 'it almost goes without question that' and 'there are those who hold the view that'.

Argument 1 – The writer's first argument in paragraph 2. It is that 'the internet is useful for our communication needs and for making social contacts'.

Counterargument 1 – Counterargument 1 is in the second part of paragraph 2. It is that 'these social contacts are the breeding ground for dishonest or even criminally-minded individuals who want to prey on the weak and vulnerable'.

The argumentative language from this paragraph is: 'others would assert that' and 'We have heard numerous stories of'.

Argument 2 – Argument 2 is in paragraph 3. It is that 'the internet gives us ready access to a great deal of information'.

Counterargument 2 – Counterargument 2 is in the second half of paragraph 3. It is that 'much of the so-called 'information' on the internet needs to be read with a critical mind'.

The argumentative language from this paragraph is: 'the double-edged sword effect of', 'there is no disputing that', 'Consider the case of ', 'one must also concede that' and '…are a particular worry'.

Synthesis – The synthesis of the essay is found in the first half of the last paragraph. It is 'But what about the minority of people who do not [know what is dangerous]? Will they remain unprotected just to accommodate the desires of the majority?'

Conclusion – The writer's conclusion is: 'The internet will need to face governmental regulation in the future, but that regulation will need to be moderate, because if the internet becomes too highly regulated, it will lose a great deal of the convenience that it already affords us'.

Analysis of Linking Words and Verbs in Sample Essay 4

Pay particular attention to the highlighted **linking words**, *adjectives* and <u>verbs</u> in sample essay 4 below.

In today's digital and electronic age, it almost goes without question that the internet is *practical* for our daily lives because it makes some mundane tasks more convenient. **For instance**, gone are the days when one had to go to the travel agent and sit in front of a desk while the agent looked through offers on his or her screen. Internet users can now book airline tickets and make travel arrangements in the comfort of their own living rooms with the click of a mouse. **But in spite of** the numerous conveniences of the internet, there are those who <u>hold</u> the view that the internet contains a great deal of *worthless*, *harmful* and *offensive* information and that the internet can be used to <u>perpetrate</u> deception and even crime. It appears that **although** the internet can be a *useful* tool in many ways, it needs to be used cautiously, and should even be regulated, in some circumstances.

It is an *undeniable* facet of modern life that the internet is useful for our communication needs and for making social contacts. Remember the days when one had to post a letter to communicate with someone overseas? Those days are in the past now thanks to the wonder of electronic mail, instant messaging, chat-rooms, forums and social networking sites. **Still**, others would <u>maintain</u> that often these social contacts are the breeding ground for *dishonest* or even *criminally-minded* individuals who want to prey on the weak and vulnerable. We have heard numerous stories of adolescents who are lured away from home to meet someone that they have communicated with online. Regrettably, in the end, the person making contact turns out to be a sexual predator intent on harming the young person. Such an experience, certainly, would negatively influence the child during the formative years of his or her personality development.

In addition to the double-edged sword effect of the communications capabilities of the internet, there is no disputing that the internet gives us ready access to a great deal of information. **Indeed**, some websites contain *indispensable* factual information for daily life and health. Consider the case of someone who wants to quit smoking. He or she can go to websites like the one run by the NHS to get the help and support needed to give up. Many of these types of websites are established by governmental agencies or charitable organizations, **so** the user can be confident that the information contained on these sites is *trustworthy*. **On the other hand**, **however**, one must also concede that much of the so-called 'information' on the internet needs to be read with a *critical* mind. **Since** anyone can set up a website, the qualifications of the site owner, **as well as** the accuracy and quality of the information on the site need to be perused sceptically. The rise of medical forums run by people with no medical training whatsoever and the abundance of online shops selling discount medications are a particular worry, **as** some people will rely on these websites to make a self-diagnosis and then purchase medicine, without taking heed of the possibility that the medicine could potentially kill them.

Yet, others would suggest that the media has seriously exaggerated the number of incidents of internet users being grievously harmed or killed by people they have met or products they have purchased on the internet and that the very large majority of the population have the common sense to know what is dangerous or not. But what about the minority of people who do not? Will they remain unprotected just to accommodate the desires of the majority? It is true that internet usage needs to be approached vigilantly on certain occasions. The internet will need to face governmental regulation in the future, but that regulation would need to be *moderate*, **because** if the internet becomes too highly regulated, it will lose a great deal of the convenience that it already affords us.

Analysis of Modality and Qualifiers in Sample Essay 4

Now look at essay 4 again, noting the use of <u>modality</u> and **qualifiers**.

In today's digital and electronic age, it almost goes without question that the internet is practical for our daily lives because it makes some mundane tasks more convenient. For instance, gone are the days when one had to go to the travel agent and sit in front of a desk while the agent looked through offers on his or her screen. Internet users can now book airline tickets and make travel arrangements in the comfort of their own living rooms with the click of a mouse. But in spite of the numerous conveniences of the internet, there are those who hold the view that the internet contains a great deal of worthless, harmful and offensive information and that the internet <u>can</u> be used to perpetrate deception and even crime. It appears that although the internet <u>can</u> be a useful tool in many ways, it needs to be used cautiously, and <u>should</u> even be regulated, in some circumstances.

It is an undeniable facet of modern life that the internet is useful for our communication needs and for making social contacts. Remember the days when one had to post a letter to communicate with someone overseas? Those days are in the past now thanks to the wonder of electronic mail, instant messaging, chat-rooms, forums and social networking sites. Still, others <u>would</u> maintain that often these social contacts are the breeding ground for dishonest or even criminally-minded individuals who want to prey on the weak and vulnerable. We have heard numerous stories of adolescents who are lured away from home to meet someone that they have communicated with online. **Regrettably**, in the end, the person making contact turns out to be a sexual predator intent on harming the young person. Such an experience, **certainly**, would negatively influence the child during the formative years of his or her personality development.

In addition to the double-edged sword effect of the communications capabilities of the internet, there is no disputing that the internet gives us ready access to a great deal of information. Indeed, some websites contain indispensable factual information for daily life and health. Consider the case of someone who wants to quit smoking. He or she can go to websites like the one run by the NHS to get the help and support needed to give up. Many of these types of websites are established by governmental agencies or charitable organizations, so the user can be confident that the information contained on these sites is trustworthy. On the other hand, however, one must also concede that much of the so-called 'information' on the internet needs to be read with a critical mind. Since anyone can set up a website, the qualifications of the site owner, as well as the accuracy and quality of the information on the site need to be perused sceptically. The rise of medical forums run by people with no medical training whatsoever and the abundance of online shops selling discount medications are a particular worry, as some people will rely on these websites to make a self-diagnosis and then purchase medicine, without taking heed of the possibility that the medicine could potentially kill them.

Yet, others would suggest that the media has seriously exaggerated the number of incidents of internet users being grievously harmed or killed by people they have met or products they have purchased on the internet and that the very large majority of the population have the common sense to know what is dangerous or not. But what about the minority of people who do not? Will they remain unprotected just to accommodate the desires of the majority? It is true that internet usage needs to be approached vigilantly on certain occasions. The internet will need to face governmental regulation in the future, but that regulation will need to be moderate, because if the internet becomes too highly regulated, it will lose a great deal of the convenience that it already affords us.

LNAT Practice Test 3

Section B: Essay

Allow 40 minutes to take this test. A model response to question 3 is provided in the next section.

Answer ONE of the following questions.

You must substantiate your argument with persuasive reasons and examples which justify your point of view.

1. What is your response to the following statement: 'Teenagers nowadays should be required to do a stint of manual labour to show them what a hard day's work is'.

2. The ban on cigarette smoking in public places should be repealed as it is yet another example of nanny-state politics. Discuss.

3. Euthanasia should be considered to be a basic human right. Do you agree?

Sample Essay 5

This essay is in response to essay question 3 from practice test 3 on the previous page. A detailed analysis of the essay is provided after the written essay response.

Euthanasia should be considered to be a basic human right. Do you agree?

Modern advancements in science and medicine have meant that life expectancy is much longer now than in the past. A number of previously fatal conditions and illness, such as having the HIV virus, can now be addressed with the use of medications and other treatments because of modern science. Yet, in some cases, the life that the seriously ill person lives is full of pain and suffering. Would it be more humane in these cases to permit euthanasia? The choice about receiving medical treatment or not during life-threatening conditions is one that ought to be very strictly controlled and is one that can be answered competently only if we first respond to two other questions: Who should decide what the best course of action is in each individual case and under what conditions?

Clearly, pain and suffering are very individual and private experiences as each person has a very different threshold for and tolerance of pain. Patients who have been diagnosed with terminal, incurable illnesses and have been given months to live might prefer not to live during those remaining months if there is going to be a great deal of intense suffering. In essence, the question revolves around the quality of the patient's remaining life. Nevertheless, opponents to this viewpoint are quick to point out that misdiagnoses are made and that patients do sometimes make unexplained recoveries after having received grim prognoses. But experience tells us that this is normally not the case: miraculous recoveries are few and far between in reality, and having false hope generally only works to prolong suffering and a poor quality of life.

The 'quality of life' argument is particularly persuasive when the patient shows no brain activity and is being kept alive on a life support machine. If our loved one is mentally incapacitated, he or she cannot make a decision about his or her own welfare. Who then should? Is it right for family members to decide? The problem is that family members, already struggling to come to terms with their loved one's grave condition, are now placed in the unenviable position of having to make an agonizing choice. They may ask themselves what their loved one would have wanted, but in the end, such decisions are made under great mental duress and may be decisions that the family members ultimately live to regret.

However, the argument above is based on the presumption that the family relationship is amicable and that family members will always place a priority on the wishes of their loved one. What happens when this is not the case? In the most extreme case, this argument holds that family members might act to hasten the death of the patient in order to put an end to an acrimonious family life, to be able to collect inheritance and insurance pay-outs, or both. Avarice, they claim, is a more powerful human motivator than love, so consider the power of greed when love has ceased to exist. Surely, they assert, we should not let those who stand to gain from the patient's death make the very decision that the patient should die.

In order to attempt to address the murky issues surrounding euthanasia, several countries are now recognizing Advance Health Directives as a matter of law. The directive, which the individual must make when he or she is of sound mind, stipulates the conditions for the receipt of medical treatment and hospital care. The legal document must be signed and sworn and is valid only when and if the person giving the directive is unable to provide consent because of mental incapacity. Such a document effectively removes the need for family members to ponder the wishes of the patient since the patient has already committed his or her wishes to writing. The document also protects the patient in the event that unscrupulous family members may want to hasten the patient's death for personal or financial reasons. While the debate about euthanasia *per se* might continue in cases where the patient has not expressed his or her wishes beforehand, Advance Health Directives are certainly a positive step in addressing the issue. [689 words]

Analysis of Essay Structure in Sample Essay 5

The structure of the essay and the argumentative language the essay uses are analysed below. On the following pages, the writer's use of linking words, adjectives, modality, qualifiers and verbs is analysed.

This essay uses a 'scheme 2' organizational scheme.

Assertion – The primary assertion is in the last sentence of paragraph 1: 'The choice about receiving medical treatment or not during life-threatening conditions is one that ought to be very strictly controlled and is one that can be answered competently only if we first respond to two other questions: Who should decide what the best course of action is in each individual case and under what conditions?'

The argumentative language from this paragraph is: 'have meant that' and 'in some cases'.

Argument 1 – The writer's first argument in paragraph 2. It is that 'Patients who have been diagnosed with terminal, incurable illnesses and have been given months to live might prefer not to live during those remaining months if there is going to be a great deal of intense suffering'.

Counterargument 1 – Counterargument 1 is in the second half of paragraph 2. It is that 'misdiagnoses are made and that patients do sometimes make unexplained recoveries after having received grim prognoses'.

The argumentative language from this paragraph is: 'the question revolves around', 'opponents to this viewpoint', 'experience tells us that', 'so-called' and 'in reality'.

Argument 2 – Argument 2 is in paragraph 3. It is that the "quality of life' argument is particularly persuasive when the patient shows no brain activity and is being kept alive on a life support machine'.

The argumentative language from this paragraph is: 'argument is particularly persuasive when', 'Is it right for ... to ...?', 'The problem is that' and 'They may ask themselves'.

Counterargument 2 – Counterargument 2 is in paragraph 4. It is that there are flaws in the argument that 'the family relationship is amicable and that family members will always place a priority on the wishes of their loved one'.

The argumentative language from this paragraph is: 'the argument above is based on the presumption that...', 'What happens when this is not the case?', 'In the most extreme case', 'this argument holds that...', 'they claim', 'so consider' and 'they assert'.

Synthesis – The synthesis of the essay is found in the last paragraph. It is that 'In order to attempt to address the murky issues surrounding euthanasia, several countries are now recognizing Advance Health Directives as a matter of law'.

Conclusion – The writer's conclusion is: 'While the debate about euthanasia *per se* might continue in cases where the patient has not expressed his or her wishes beforehand, Advance Health Directives are certainly a positive step in addressing the issue'.

Analysis of Linking Words and Verbs in Sample Essay 5

Pay particular attention to the highlighted **linking words**, *adjectives* and <u>verbs</u> in sample essay 5 below.

Modern advancements in science and medicine have meant that life expectancy is much longer now than in the past. A number of previously fatal conditions and illness, such as having the HIV virus, can now be addressed with the use of medications and other treatments because of modern science. **Yet**, in some cases, the life that the seriously ill person lives is full of pain and suffering. Would it be more humane in these cases to permit euthanasia? The choice about receiving medical treatment or not during life-threatening conditions is one that ought to be very strictly controlled and is one that can be answered competently only if we **first** respond to two other questions: Who should decide what the *best* course of action is in each individual case and under what conditions?

Clearly, pain and suffering are very *individual* and *private* experiences as each person has a very *different* threshold for and tolerance of pain. Patients who have been diagnosed with terminal, incurable illnesses and have been given months to live might prefer not to live during those remaining months if there is going to be a great deal of *intense* suffering. **In essence**, the question revolves around the quality of the patient's remaining life. **Nevertheless**, opponents to this viewpoint are quick to point out that misdiagnoses are made and that patients do sometimes make unexplained recoveries after having received *grim* prognoses. But experience tells us that this is normally not the case: miraculous recoveries are few and far between in reality, and having false hope generally only works to prolong suffering and a *poor* quality of life.

The 'quality of life' argument is particularly *persuasive* **when** the patient shows no brain activity and is being kept alive on a life support machine. If our loved one is mentally incapacitated, he or she cannot make a decision about his or her own welfare. Who then should? Is it right for family members to decide? The problem is that family members, already struggling to come to terms with their loved one's *grave* condition, are now placed in the *unenviable* position of having to make an *agonizing* choice. They may ask themselves what their loved one would have wanted, but in the end, such decisions are made under great mental duress and may be decisions that the family members ultimately live to regret.

However, the argument above is based on the presumption that the family relationship is *amicable* and that family members will always place a priority on the wishes of their loved one. What happens when this is not the case? In the most extreme case, this argument holds that family members might act to hasten the death of the patient in order to put an end to an *acrimonious* family life, to be able to collect inheritance and insurance pay-outs, or both. Avarice, they claim, is a more powerful human motivator than love, **so** consider the power of greed when love has ceased to exist. Surely, they assert, we should not let those who stand to gain from the patient's death make the very decision that the patient should die.

In order to attempt to address the *murky* issues surrounding euthanasia, several countries are now recognizing Advance Health Directives as a matter of law. The directive, which the individual must make when he or she is of sound mind, stipulates the conditions for the receipt of medical treatment and hospital care. The legal document must be signed and sworn and is valid only when and if the person giving the directive is unable to provide consent **because of** mental incapacity. Such a document effectively removes the need for family members to ponder the wishes of the patient **since** the patient has already committed his or her wishes to writing. The document **also** protects the patient in the event that *unscrupulous* family members may want to hasten the patient's death for personal or financial reasons. **While** the debate about euthanasia per se might continue in cases where the patient has not expressed his or her wishes beforehand, Advance Health Directives are certainly a *positive* step in addressing the issue.

Analysis of Modality and Qualifiers in Sample Essay 5

Now look at essay 5 again, noting the use of <u>modality</u> and **qualifiers**.

Modern advancements in science and medicine have meant that life expectancy is much longer now than in the past. A number of previously fatal conditions and illness, such as having the HIV virus, can now be addressed with the use of medications and other treatments because of modern science. Yet, in some cases, the life that the seriously ill person lives is full of pain and suffering. <u>Would</u> it be more humane in these cases to permit euthanasia? The choice about receiving medical treatment or not during life-threatening conditions is one that <u>ought</u> to be very strictly controlled and is one that can be answered competently only if we first respond to two other questions: Who <u>should</u> decide what the best course of action is in each individual case and under what conditions?

Clearly, pain and suffering are very individual and private experiences as each person has a very different threshold for and tolerance of pain. Patients who have been diagnosed with terminal, incurable illnesses and have been given months to live <u>might</u> prefer not to live during those remaining months if there is going to be a great deal of intense suffering. In essence, the question revolves around the quality of the patient's remaining life. Nevertheless, opponents to this viewpoint are quick to point out that misdiagnoses are made and that patients do sometimes make unexplained recoveries after having received grim prognoses. But experience tells us that this is normally not the case: miraculous recoveries are few and far between in reality, and having false hope generally only works to prolong suffering and a poor quality of life.

The 'quality of life' argument is **particularly** persuasive when the patient shows no brain activity and is being kept alive on a life support machine. If our loved one is mentally incapacitated, he or she cannot make a decision about his or her own welfare. Who then should? Is it right for family members to decide? The problem is that family members, already struggling to come to terms with their loved one's grave condition, are now placed in the unenviable position of having to make an agonizing choice. They may ask themselves what their loved one would have wanted, but in the end, such decisions are made under great mental duress and may be decisions that the family members ultimately live to regret.

However, the argument above is based on the presumption that the family relationship is amicable and that family members will always place a priority on the wishes of their loved one. What happens when this is not the case? In the most extreme case, this argument holds that family members might act to hasten the death of the patient in order to put an end to an acrimonious family life, to be able to collect inheritance and insurance pay-outs, or both. Avarice, they claim, is a more powerful human motivator than love, so consider the power of greed when love has ceased to exist. Surely, they assert, we should not let those who stand to gain from the patient's death make the very decision that the patient <u>should</u> die.

In order to attempt to address the murky issues surrounding euthanasia, several countries are now recognizing Advance Health Directives as a matter of law. The directive, which the individual <u>must</u> make when he or she is of sound mind, stipulates the conditions for the receipt of medical treatment and hospital care. The legal document <u>must</u> be signed and sworn and is valid only when and if the person giving the directive is unable to provide consent because of mental incapacity. Such a document effectively removes the need for family members to ponder the wishes of the patient since the patient has already committed his or her wishes to writing. The document also protects the patient in the event that unscrupulous family members <u>may</u> want to hasten the patient's death for personal or financial reasons. While the debate about euthanasia per se <u>might</u> continue in cases where the patient has not expressed his or her wishes beforehand, Advance Health Directives are **certainly** a positive step in addressing the issue.

LNAT Practice Test 4

Section B: Essay

Answer ONE of the following questions.

You must substantiate your argument with persuasive reasons and examples which justify your point of view.

1. All animal testing for scientific reasons should be banned. Discuss.

2. What is your response to the view that the death penalty should be reinstated for all those convicted of murder?

3. Boarding schools help children to grow into well-adjusted adults. Do you agree?

LNAT Practice Test 5

Section B: Essay

Answer ONE of the following questions.

You must substantiate your argument with persuasive reasons and examples which justify your point of view.

1. The government should do more to address the issue of domestic violence. Do you agree?

2. Society is becoming increasingly reliant on computers for communication. Is this a good thing?

3. Censorship in printed and digital media should be considered a necessary evil. Discuss.

www.ingramcontent.com/pod-product-compliance
Lightning Source LLC
Chambersburg PA
CBHW081353080526
44588CB00016B/2486